CW01635465

Dear Son Barr,

If you have nothing better to
come with me and pay a visit to the " Drury
of the East," otherwise, the Brittania
e, Hoxton; a theatre better known to the
tants of that salubrious locality as,
rit'", " the good old Brit'," or " The
Brit'. The last term of endearment being
ause of the many "Blood and Thunder" "Bello-"
at were prdduced there - to name but one,
Todd the Demon Barber of Fleet Street, or
of Pearls."
re, in High Street, Hoxton; a narrow,
l-paved thouroughfare, with countless
ng the gutters - a street - shrieking wi
rr of sweat shop wheels, and the raucous
stone vendors, - a street - crowded with
urous, unclean children, hanging on to
il skirts of frowsy females, who fill
the cell-like compartments of the
Children packed like sardines into
d perambulators, two and three to a

ly pieces of newspaper;-
th upon pigs feet or
m their dirty digits,
aste called musical
ing publicly in the
children dancing in the
row of an asthmatic
howling, yelling, scream-
ing, crawling; - children

count as

3

's! At the mere mention of that
ction wanders back to the period
fancy. Let us look in the window.
d shop still retains its old time
- look! There's a similar toy sta
you have - a replica of the one I h
the same gaudy coloured, highly var
enium, with the early Victorian
ladies and the frill shirted gentry,
f the stage boxes, - the same long
and bewhiskered left handed musician
stra, - the same red linen act drop -
ats " - figure slides, the traps,
ron and scenery - nothing has altered
dboard characters, who stand in ex-
es in their tin slides upon the
are the pasteboard actors de-
The Pirates Lair." Penny plain
- no - nothing has changed, not
a coloured woodcut of your
- another of your grandfather
the border?
Clown "
Harlequin"
atre Pantomime -
e - 187-.
ave been connected
eatre for near

f sa
green cabbag
Ah! - we're there - ju
- the Bleedin' Brit!!! -
! There's a depressing atmosphere
place. The once bright lights have gone, so have
highly coloured six-sheets; there are no crowds
ghting their way in, gone are the " chuckers-out"
f herculean proportions, who used to keep order
favour or affection; there is no whitewash

Brick-Dust Rouge

Painting by G. B. Lupino Jnr., 1981

Brick-Dust Rouge
A Letter to My Son
New York, 1927

A beautiful, charming and moving piece of writing from not only a truly masterful exponent of words but a highly respected man of his time.

George Barry Lupino Senior

Edited and with a foreword by
Janet Lupino

ASPECT

A Letter to My Son
George Barry Lupino Senior

Published by Aspect Design, 2018

Designed, printed and bound by Aspect Design
89 Newtown Road, Malvern, Worcs. WR14 1PD
United Kingdom
Tel: 01684 561567
E-mail: allan@aspect-design.net
Website: www.aspect-design.net

A copy of this book has been deposited
with the British Library Board

ISBN 978-1-912078-96-7

In memory of my dear husband,
G. B. Lupino Jnr.,
and his father, G. B. Lupino Snr.

'Encouragement promotes ingenious performance'
(The Lupino family motto)

Lupino coat of arms designed by G. B. Lupino Snr.

A BRIEF HISTORY OF THE LUPINOS
known as 'The Royal Family of Greasepaint'

In the early 1600s Georguis Luppino stepped onto the safety of English soil after sailing from Italy. He fled the life of a performer, actor, and acrobat having become a political refugee for expressing opinions contrary to those espoused by the political powers of the day. Sadly, his wife died during the journey leaving him with a baby boy to look after and his precious collection of life-sized puppets.

He managed to keep the two of them alive and found that the puppets were a godsend and trained his son to help him. The puppet show was seen in open markets even though Cromwell closed all theatres not showing religious plays. Georguis continued entertaining the crowds around the country and when King Charles II was returned to the throne, the Luppinos were granted licences to play in the service of the king at the Drury Lane theatre, little knowing that three hundred years later the Lupino family would be given the title of 'the royal family of greasepaint'.

Through the centuries, the name Luppino became Lupino with one *p*. They trained to perform as animals, acrobats, actors, dancers, trapeze artists, and tightrope walkers, as well as being artistically gifted as painters who were responsible for creating the scenery for shows in the theatrical world. Most of all they were famous for their humorous appearances as clowns, and later as Dames in the pantomimes, and in music hall and musical shows which were such a success in America.

However, the height of their success was undoubtedly during the first half of the twentieth century when their names were seen on billboards in London and other major cities in different productions and films. The true characters and stories concerning the family are hilarious. George, Harry, Barry, Mark, Stanley, Lupino Lane, Wallace, Ida, Laurie and Barry Jnr. and more, all contributed to a legacy that should not be forgotten. Hence adding another accolade to their name 'the oldest theatrical family in the world'.

Janet Lupino

FOREWORD

Sometime after the death of my husband, George Barry Lupino Jnr., in 1995, I decided to open up an old chest that had previously always travelled with the family and was unceremoniously tucked away to avoid occupying space, with little attention given to it. You cannot imagine, when my children and I eventually opened up the chest, our surprise to discover an 'Aladdin's Cave' of theatrical memorabilia, some of which dated back three hundred years or more.

Inside there was an amazing number of old scripts and information, both typed and hand-written of various different pantomimes, musical comedy shows, comedy scenes and gags along with detailed drawings of acrobatic tricks describing for instance how trap doors were used in the hilarious and famous 'Lupino Chases' that left audiences shrieking with laughter. Over time, the Lupinos became known professionally as the oldest theatrical family in the world and given the title of 'the royal family of greasepaint'.

Amongst the many articles we found a forty-five page letter from George Barry Lupino Snr., my husband's father, dated Christmas 1927. It is this letter that is reproduced in this book. He describes the life in which he grew up within the sound of Bow Bells in the East End of London in the late 1800s. This letter was written when he was performing in America in 1927 and gives amazingly detailed information about the people, the places, the sights, sounds, and smells of the East End of London and Drury Lane at the height of the Britannia Theatre's popularity during the 1880s to 1890s.

He describes the music hall stars and characters of the era and the hilarious tricks and pranks in which he and his brother were involved. He was familiar with the famous Sarah Lane who ran the Britannia Theatre, Hoxton, and managed the actors and performers with a rod of iron.

Because the characters and activities within the letter are so well described with such feeling for the atmosphere of that period, we invite you to join us and be transported with him to that time and place.

Janet Lupino

Dear Reader,

Overleaf is a very brief history of the Britannia Theatre, Hoxton, which I have written to provide you with a better understanding of the following letter. As far as the letter is concerned, I have strictly adhered to its original presentation to preserve the letter's authenticity.

As you may not be familiar with some of the archaic terminology, it was decided that a few well-placed footnotes would aid your understanding and make it a more pleasurable read. However, you may want to further research the characters, places, names and dates for yourselves, which I highly recommend.

Janet Lupino

A Very Brief History of the Britannia Theatre, Hoxton

The Britannia Theatre, Hoxton, was built in 1858 by Sam Lane on the site of two buildings he owned previously, called the Britannia Tavern and the Britannia Saloon respectively. These entertainment venues were extremely popular with the local community. The two buildings were demolished to make way for a much larger single venue with 3,250 seats. Including standing room it was capable of accommodating an audience of over four thousand.

The newly built Britannia Theatre attracted great stars such as Vesta Tilley, George Lupino, Lupino Lane, Dan Leno, Arthur Lloyd and many more.

When Sam died in 1871 he bequeathed the Britannia to his wife, Sarah Lane, whose performances had already made her a great favourite with the public and was known as the 'Queen of Hoxton'. Sarah died in 1898 and the theatre was sold to the Gaumont Film Company and continued as a cinema until the Second World War when it was destroyed by bombing during the Blitz, c. 1940.

G. B. Lupino Snr. c. 1927, when he wrote the letter to his son.

G. B. Lupino Jnr. c. 1927, when his father wrote this letter.

New York,
Xmas, 1927

My dear son, Barry,

If you have nothing better to do, come with me and pay a visit to the 'Drury Lane of the East,' otherwise, the Britannia Theatre, Hoxton; a theatre better known to the inhabitants of that salubrious locality as 'the Brit', 'the good old Brit', or 'the bleedin' Brit'. The last term of endearment being used because of the many 'Blood and Thunder' 'Bello' dramas that were produced there – to name but one, *Sweeney Todd the Demon Barber of Fleet Street, or the String of Pearls.*

Here we are, in High Street, Hoxton; a narrow, winding, ill-paved thoroughfare, with countless barrows lining the gutters – a street – shrieking with the whirr of sweat shop wheels, and the raucous rant of kerb-stone vendors – a street – crowded with gangs of clamorous, unclean children, hanging on to the draggle-tail skirts of frowsy females, who fill to overflowing the cell-like compartments of the numerous 'pubs'. Children packed like sardines into bent and battered perambulators, two and three to a seat – children in push chairs, go-carts, in sugar crates – children sucking sickly looking sugar sticks, lumps of nauseous nougat, hunks of hard-bake – children chewing chunks of bread and jam – eating fish and chips from oily newspaper – children cutting their milk teeth upon pigs feet or pickles – children licking from their dirty digits, a loathsome saffron coloured paste called musical pastry; children in arms dining publicly in the manner ordered by nature, children dancing in the roadway to the ear-splitting row of an asthmatic barrel organ; – children howling, yelling, screaming, fighting, biting, kicking, crawling – children here, there – everywhere!

What a street! – a place where one can count as Coleridge says; 'Two and seventy stenches, all well-defined – and several stinks' – or, if you prefer Shakespeare's; 'An ancient fish-like smell.' The whole locality reeks, positively reeks with the acrid aroma of rancid fried fish fat, stale beer, costermonger garbage, and the penetrating, pungent smell of the great unwashed.

But there – you would come;

The Brit opens its doors at six thirty so we had better hurry, for we have yet a tidy step to travel before we get there – now! What have you found? Pollock's – well – er – perhaps we can spare a few moments for Pollock's.[1]

Pollock's! At the mere mention of that name, our recollection wanders back to the period of innocent infancy. Let us look in the window. Ah! Yes, the old shop retains its old time fascination – look! There's a similar toy stage to the one you have – a replica of the one I had as a boy – the same gaudy coloured, highly varnished proscenium, with the early Victorian ermine clad ladies and the frill shirted gentry gazing out of the stage boxes – the same long, curly-haired and be-whiskered left-handed musicians in the orchestra – the same red linen act drop – the tin 'floats' – figure slides, the traps, grooves, gridiron and scenery – nothing has altered, not even the cardboard characters, who stand in exaggerated attitudes in their tin slides upon the stage – what piece are the pasteboard actors depicting? *Alone in the Pirate's Lair.* Penny plain and two pence coloured – no – nothing has changed, not even the price.

Oh, Look! Look! There's a coloured woodcut of your great grandfather – and see – another of your grandfather – what does the printing say on the border?

'George Lupino Snr., Clown.'

'George Lupino Jnr., Harlequin.'

1 Benjamin Pollock's toy theatre shop was situated close to Drury Lane.

What else – 'In the Britannia Theatre Pantomime' – 'The Black Statue', and the date – 1871.

1871! Just imagine! The Lupinos have been connected with this neighbourhood and that theatre for nearly sixty years, which reminds me – we had better get along to the theatre – come on!

Ah! The street begins to get wider, we are approaching that temple of Thespis where so many of our family 'once did strut and fret' their hour upon the stage. Yes, there's Pimlico Walk, that narrow alley, down which I have often walked, with my Saturday penny to buy a half-penny glass of raspberry at Dalmaine's, the tooth extractor. Here's the old corner junk shop, with its overflow of bedsteads, chests of drawers, kitchen utensils, and other second-hand debris oozing out on to the pavement. Now comes the baker's where I used to buy a ha'porth of stale rock cakes to eke out the 'cut from the joint' and 'two veg' from the 'good pull up for carmen' opposite – Grr! I can taste that mid-show meal yet – tasteless, anaemic beef, floating in a pool of saffron coloured iodiform – a slab of emerald green cabbage – and an almost petrified spud – Grr! – Ah! – we're there – the Brit! – the good old Brit!! – the bleedin' Brit!!! – just the same – no it isn't!! There's a depressing atmosphere hanging over the place. The once bright lights have gone, so have the highly coloured six-sheets;[2] there are no crowds fighting their way in, gone are the 'chuckers-out' of herculean proportions, who used to keep order without favour or affection; there is no whitewash or sawdust on the steps of the saloon bar – in fact there is no saloon – there is no Brit.

All that is left is a huge mass of decaying brick, warping and sun-blistered doors; a row of bent and battered brass lamps, covered in Verdigris, behind cracked and grimy plate glass windows – nothing but a memory.

One solitary arc lamp splutters and spits in the hallway of what once was the entrance to the stalls – outside on the kerb stands

[2] Six-sheets were posters 1,200 mm x 1,800 mm in size and were popular with theatres and cinemas.

a solitary, cadaverous individual, dressed in a frayed and filthy beer stained uniform – trying his best to attract the custom of a group of gutter snipes, who pay scant attention to his mournful cry, 'The feature film is now showing'

The saloon bar depresses me more than anything else – that once bright and cheery place is now a storeroom for broken furniture – what a cosy, delightful bar it used to be – in my mind's eye I can see the well-polished pewter mugs hanging from the shelves covered with bright tumblers, surrounded by large, juicy oranges and lemons. The highly polished counter with the painted china beer pullers – the round of beef – what a size the ox must have been – I used to think, as I would contemplate the huge willow pattern plate that seemed almost to groan beneath the weight; – the buckhorn carver and fork protruding from its side, the parsley displayed to impart a zest – as if any were needed in those hungry days; – the jars of pickles, the home-made bread, the huge cheese, the glass jars containing assorted cakes and banburys – the gleaming mirrors decorated with the whitewash announcements about the Goose Club; the great Buffalo Horns with R.A.O.B. sign forming the centre of the attraction; the photograph-covered walls – and presiding over all Sam Crawford.[3]

What memories that name conjures up – I can see them all, Uncle Sam, Aunt Fanny, Cousin Sam, Bert, Artie, Lilly, the boys somewhat patronizing, because their father was Mrs Lane's nephew, Lily retiring and unapproachable. Aunty Fanny with the grand manner who never seemed to forget the fact that she was the beauty of the tribe, and had married a Crawford with expectations from Aunt Sarah – Uncle Sam, proud and portly, with his close trimmed beard, looking like a King Edward V!!

3 The Goose Club was a scheme whereby people could pay small sums in advance to save enough to buy a Christmas goose.

R.O.A.B. – the Royal Antediluvian Order of Buffaloes, the association formed by those associated with the theatre including actors and stagehands.

turned publican; serving pots of four ale with the dignity of a dean, smoking a pipe of huge dimensions, with mountains of silver, a plate of which precious metal acquainted the curious, that it had been presented to him by his brother-in-law, George Lupino, on the interesting occasion of his marriage. How gleaming white the Saturday night shirt used to appear, how the diamond decorated masonic emblem on his immense gold watch chain, used to fascinate me. My Uncle Sam, my rich uncle, who would occasionally give me an art cake with the manners of a mayor presenting the freedom of the city.

In fancy I can see the tall wooden stool upon which I used to sit, hour after hour, waiting for Dad to go home, wriggling about with childish restlessness – and by so wriggling – gradually imparting a silk-like sheen to the seat of my Fauntleroys;[4] wriggling and twisting about until nature would no longer be denied, and I would fall asleep with my head resting against the spiral iron staircase, only to awaken when those wonderful words, 'Time, gents, please,' would ring through the smoke laden bar. The times I have counted the steps of that spiral staircase, over and over again – counting anything – everything – the number of corks, glasses, the people, the photographs – counting anything to help break the monotony of waiting and listening to the endless babble of show-shop – when I eventually tired of this occupation, I would trace with my finger the filigree decoration of the steps – and sometimes, though not often – if I were given a glass of spruce hot (a drink that was said to be good for bruises) I would, with the assistance of this 'Dutch Courage', climb cautiously and quietly up the steps until I had almost penetrated that sanctuary – the Crawford's Quarters over the Bar.

This Holy of Holies I was seldom allowed to enter, the trap door at the top usually being the limit of my explorations.

4 Fauntleroys were suits in which the Victorians liked to clothe their children, especially for photographs – so called after the novel *Little Lord Fauntleroy* by Francis Hodgson Burnett, published in 1886.

How I remember that old spiral staircase – down which in after years, Aunt Fanny was unable to come, owing to neglecting her daily dozen and not counting her calories.

It is still there, but now it is a broken mass of rusty iron and leads only to empty, dusty rooms.

Look! There's a small, iron pass door leading into the stalls bar – let us squeeze through – 'We're in, Meredith – we're in.'

See! There's Uncle Alfred – uncle only by courtesy – there he stands at the stalls entrance, dressed in his long frock coat and tall hat, looking somewhat like an undertaker upon a holiday;- taking checks from the stallites with the urbanity of a court usher – he hasn't altered a bit – even the bump over his eye is still there, how I longed, as a child, to slap that bump with a slap-stick, just to see what would happen.

Standing next to him is his assistant, an old man with a hand set into a permanent claw, through carrying, year after year, countless copper bags to the bank; -and next to him is old G. B. Bigwood – old Jimmy – (whose right name was George) – jovial James – who has been connected with the Brit almost from the day that old Sam Lane converted it from a saloon and beer garden into a regular theatre.

'Old Jimmy!' – There he is, arrayed as usual in his parsonic suit of black, tall white all round collar, black silk Oxford tie, and the out-standing feature of his make-up – a black velvet smoking cap, perched jauntily upon his white hair – watch him bow low to the customers as he ushers them up the circle steps with the courtesy of a caliph.[5] Old 'G. B. BIGWOOD' – one of the finest comedians that ever trod the boards of the old Brit.

And look! – There's old Burgess, the principal 'bouncer' – the 'chucker out,' old Burgess, the 'boy bouncer,' – in person he was large, in appearance ferocious, in height he had as much

5 'Caliph' was the title of Muslim civil and religious rulers and meant 'successor of Muhammad'. It is used here as a term of endearment.

as most men can boast of, while in rotundity he possessed more than most men care to be encumbered with. Not to be ungenerous, he was what is usually designated as fat – in fact, his circumference so increased towards the latter end of his career – that this one time King of Bouncers found himself at times subjected to impertinent remarks from some of the shirt sleeved gentry among the audience – when this occurred his be-whiskered face would assume a ferocity positively distressing to witness – then with a lion-like roar, that could be heard all over the house, entirely drowning the actors, he would push his way through the people, scattering them right and left, without fear or favour, pounce on the would-be wit, drag him back through the crowd, who would part like chaff before the wind – then Zowy! – Bump! Bump! Bump! – down the gallery steps, until a final crash of the gallery doors, three flights below, would announce to the expectant and attentive audience, that Bill Burgess had 'bounced his boy,' then, and not till then, would the gallery settle down to comparative peace as the actors resumed their interrupted dialogue.

Old Burgess! – he had only to pop his face round the corner and say – 'Shan't tell yer no more – me lads,' to obtain the quietude of a crypt.

You will notice that he has dyed his whiskers brown, or rather, mostly brown, here and there are patches of purple – how many times has Dad told him to try walnut juice – but no, he will stick to Condy's crystals. – Who is he talking to? Why, it's little old J. B. Howe, 'the Pocket Kean,' one of the greatest Shakespearean actors of the age, he also has been playing here almost as many years as old Bigwood. He is a gentleman who had the unthankful task of trying to instil the art of elocution into the ivory domes of your Uncle Mark and me. At the period of which I write, I'm afraid we paid but scant attention to his instructions, playing practical jokes upon the old boy occupied most of our time – Yes, I am sorry to say, at that time, neither your uncle nor I were what you could term – 'attractive children' – we were usually referred to as – 'the red-headed sewer rat – and the bandy brat,' what a life we used to lead him – and everyone else if it comes to that.

I remember once, after a particularly trying lesson, squeezing a plentiful supply of rubber solution into his riding boots; and I can distinctly recollect the rumpus that occurred when he tried to pull them off – his socks had set securely to the soles, with the result that the boots, – the patent leather boots, the pride of the props, had to be hacked away piece by piece. I can also call to mind the sensation that was caused when he removed his Othello tights and discovered that we had powdered the insides with lamp black – and also the effective curtain we were responsible for, to Shakespeare's Venetian Tragedy, through introducing 'sneezing powder,' under the slip of the pillow that he used to smother the fair Desdemona with. How she did sneeze – and how did he in fact, the duet became so violent, they had to lower the curtain with disastrous results, for this only served to send the powder over the footlights, to the great inconvenience of the orchestra, who were forced to join in. What a beating we got on the buttocks for this improvement upon 'the Bard.' I can feel even now the business end of the broad sword, and the flesh crushing clip on the ear from his small, but exceedingly bony hand – in fancy I can hear his dear wife, Julia Summers, pleading for leniency, 'Please, please, make due allowance for the folly of youth.'

'Youth, be damned!' – Whack! – 'the ingrates!' – Biff! Biff! – 'Avaunt and quit my sight!' – Wham! – 'Thoud fiend of Hell!' – Wallop! Wallop!! Crash!!! – Yes, I must admit we were not exactly angels in those days.

Let us join the group around the bar drinking Crawford's 'sheep-dip' that tall gentleman – the one in the top coat – with the near-sealskin collar is Algernon Sims [Syms], the Hero of Hoxton.

Goodness only knows how long he has been playing 'juvenile

George (Hook) Lupino, George Lupino Snr., New York, 1877

lead' – the elderly gentleman on his left, is his grandson; – how annoyed he was when Roy Redgrave displaced him as 'juvenile lead.'[6] The story runs that he was so upset at giving the 'heroes' up to Redgrave, that he refused to meet him at the first rehearsal and sent Jimmy Dunlop, the second comic to report upon the intruder, while he, in the meantime, swallowed the insult and other things at the Red Lion.

'Never have I been so insulted – I, Algernon Sims – THE Sims – reduced to the ranks. Bah! Here have I been playing Romeo for the past forty years – and now this young beggar steps in. Landlord! Another!! – Well, Dunlop, have you seen him? _ Yes! – What is the – er – person like? Is he – er – young? 'Young! The beggar's got teeth!'

The other tall gentlemen, the one in the shooting coat and sand shoes, is Walter Steadman, the most detested and adored man in Hoxton; he 'played the villains' – he is howled, hooted and hissed at for thirty weeks per year, and petted and presented with all kinds of presents for one.

The fat man in a cycling suit is Joe Lawrence, the principal comedian – it is said he is courting Marie Bryan, Mrs Lane's niece, some say because Marie has ex-pectations from Auntie, – but, shush! The short horsey-looking man in the blue melton box cloth coat – the one with the diamond horseshoe pin in his tie – is Edmund Edmund, of the Albert and Edmund Troupe – the other two are his brothers, Jimmy and Willie; the handsome looking man in the pearl grey frock overcoat and silk hat, is of course, your grandfather; the short, thick-set, Jewish-looking gentleman, with the military looking moustache – the one in the silk hat a trifle too small for him, is your great-grandfather – the tall thin man who is talking so much about – (I think it is a certain Nipper Lupino, who astounded the natives of Glasgow so much, that he was literally snowed under with presents) is Uncle Harry – the short, red-faced, smiling man

6 Roy Redgrave was the father of Michael Redgrave and the grandfather to Vanessa Redgrave.

with a cello, who is waiting to get a word in about Cissie, is Uncle Arthur.

It is evidently getting near the pantomime season and as you are not born yet, we will leave them – listening to dear old Uncle Harry, and take a peek at the building as it was then.

How orderly it all seems – look at those great arches, outlined with multi-coloured fairy lamps, – the gaily painted foliage that decorates the immense walls, observe, – the vine leaves and huge clusters of grapes that hang in festoons from the trellis covered ceiling. Cast your eyes on the glittering cut glass chandeliers that adorn the numerous mirrors, lending additional distance to the vast space – glance at the numerous bay trees that stand in brass bound tubs upon the snow white sanded ground.

What a bower of beauty the old Brit must have been in those days to the inhabitants of Hoxton, an absolute oasis in the desert of dirty, dilapidated tenements, squalid shops, squeezed in between narrow, noxious alleys, ankle deep in decaying refuse from hawkers stalls – a veritable Garden of Eden – breathing an atmosphere of contentment, comfort and cleanliness, combined with a slight odour of oranges and Sanitas.

The entrance fee to this Elysium was, to use language of the locality, 'the 'umble tissy' – 'the sprightly sprat' – a 'sprazie', a 'tanner' or in plain English, sixpence.

But, let us stroll round the back, this way – that vast crypt, smelling so strongly of beer, is the pit bar. No spirits allowed to be sold there – only beer, Uncle Sam won't allow competition – do you see the tin tank with the shoulder straps? – well, that is full of 'arf an' arf'. Presently, a man will strap that on, and go into the pit and gallery selling it at a penny a pot – you'll notice the pot is chained to the tank – the pit and galleryites are great souvenir hunters – and one can't be too careful, can one? – Ah! Here's the coconut matting, we've arrived at the pit stalls – round this way – mind the steps – there are four – through the iron door – here we are! The stage!!

Wait a moment until we get accustomed to the lack of light

– Ah! that's better! – I see they haven't 'set' yet, so you can get a good idea of the size of the stage – isn't it immense! – Six inches bigger than Drury Lane – just imagine – six inches bigger – my word, how proud we were of those six inches. But let us explore; first we'll try the O.P. Side[7] – see – that little room just under the stairs? – well – that used to be Mrs Lane's private room – it was known as 'The Queen's Quarters', that throne-like chair in the first entrance was hers also – here she would sit, night after night, with her bonnet be-decked head bobbing to and fro – watching with hawk-like eye for any slackness or slip-shod work, and with ears tuned in for any suggestiveness – the old Brit may have been a very rough theatre – but it was ruled with a Kaiser-like firmness – and the decencies were rigidly observed – woe betide the comic who cracked a 'cerulean[8] gag' – up would go her diamond-decked finger – and down would come the curtain, regardless of what portion of the play was in progress – 'My people shall not be insulted.' – How the comedians dreaded the tinkle, tinkle of the jet beads on her dolman that announced she was approaching. – 'Look out, lads! – Sad face Sara is coming.' No comedian was ever known to make her smile, let alone laugh.

During the performance of the show, nothing would disturb her sphinx-like calm, except when some comedian would grumble at the noisy audience, (and they could be noisy when they wanted to) to try and shout above three and four thousand people in a holiday mood required the voice of a Stentor and a Job-like disposition.

Many a comedian, just to make conversation, has remarked, 'Very noisy tonight, Mrs Lane.' 'Noisy they may be,' she would reply – 'Very noisy – and likely to be so for the next three or four months, so go and amuse them my boy – go on and earn your money, I pay you to be funny – be so.' Once she remarked to a comedian, who was somewhat confidential in method, 'Louder

7 O.P. is short for 'Opposite Prompt' which refers to the side of the stage opposite the prompt corner – traditionally situated stage left.

8 'Cerulean' means 'sky blue' and here refers to a 'blue' or risqué joke.

Sara Lane, proprietress of the Britannia Theatre, Hoxton, c. 1857.

AND Funnier.' Temperamental tantrums were not tolerated under any circumstances – fainting fits – tired tonsils – aching ankles – hoarseness – irritation, arguments and matinee moods, were conspicuous by their absence, I remember – because two rival comics had agreed to disagree, she put up the notice and the pantomime had only been running a week or so – and the usual run was any period from twelve to eighteen weeks – nothing was said – the show finished, back came the stock company and everything went on as if nothing unusual had occurred. Strange to relate, both the comedians were re-engaged for the next season, but this pantomime, they made that celebrated double act 'David and Jonothan,' look like the Two Macs.

Yes, there was only one 'boss' in that theatre – Mrs Sara Lane – how she ever put up with your Uncle Mark and I – goodness only knows – possibly it was because she worshipped your grandfather. 'My George,' she would say – 'My George is the finest acting pantomimist and dancer in the world.' She would always hold him up as a shining example to the company.

'My George is never late, never absent, always attentive, never slacks – and look – just look at the control he has over my public – he has only to hold up his finger to obtain absolute silence – and how my people adore him' – and they did, the house could be in an uproar – but Dad had only to make his entrance to obtain complete control; his reception on a first night was stupendous – he usually made his first appearance as some weird and wonderful pantomime creature, such as a hunch-back king, who, for misconduct in Fairyland, has been doomed by the Fairy Queen, to sleep embedded in a cavern for a thousand years or until some chosen mortal should speak certain magic words that would bring him to life – this theme varied only slightly year by year – the actual manner of his entrance seldom. The lights would go down and the principal girl would enter very timidly down the rocks until she reached a huge mass of broken stone in the centre – mysterious music would play very softly until she spoke the magic words: 'To do my bidding – I wish you here – King Krooked – King Krooked – appear! Appear!' The music would swell – the thunder roll would crash – the lightning flash – the rocks in the centre would split asunder – then silence – slowly a pin focus would pick out a huddled form crouched on a rock; but not a sound could be heard from the audience, they knew who it was – it was George!! – but they were waiting for their cue and now a word would be said, or a hand lifted until after various grimaces, stretchings, and blinking of eyes, he would say: 'Oh, me! Oh, my! Oh, me! Oh, me! Oh, me! Oh, my!' Then the house would come in – Cheer! How they would cheer, howl, applaud and shout: 'Bravo, George! – Stick it, George! – Good old George!' for minutes at a time, it was stupendous – the volume of sound, the feet stamping, the whistling and the hand clapping was positively deafening. His benefit night reception was once timed by a stopwatch – and it lasted for twelve minutes – and this is a fact – not fancy.

If there was ever a public idol among the theatre going public, George Lupino was it, and his power over the people was nothing short of marvellous – as he had only to put up his hand to quell immediately the most unruly audience that ever visited the theatre. One night, the traps would not work – something had gone wrong in the cellar, and the people who thought the trap scene one of the most important scenes in the pantomime, refused to let the pantomime continue – the entire house of nearly four thousand people, started to shout and stamp their feet in unison – Thud! Thud! Thud! – Traps! Traps! Traps! Then Wam!! – came a quart pot on the stage and things began to look dangerous. Then Dad walked on, took off his wig, held up his hand and the entire audience became as quiet as mice. 'Boys and girls,' he said, 'Boys and girls, I cannot call you ladies and gentlemen – I have known you too long.' – Here a voice from the gallery shouted, 'Good old George,' and the house started to applaud. When he had obtained silence again, he continued, 'The traps won't work, and I am not going to break my neck for a set of bloody fools. Goodnight!' and off he went, and then, how they cheered – they cheered and cheered and cheered again. So back he came – bowed and walked off and then the pantomime continued as if nothing had happened.

This is but one instance – I could name a dozen – nay a score or so – but they would take too long in the telling, so we will continue on with our explorations. Let me see, where were we? – oh, yes, in the O.P. entrance, let us go up the stairs to the gentlemen dressing room.

Here we are! – What! This narrow white washed passage isn't a dressing room – yes it is, all the principal men dress here! Eh! – there's not room for two people to pass? – What does that matter, one can sit on the bench while the other squeezes past – besides there's nowhere else to dress except the cellar – and the supers dress there. There are no windows? – Well, you can push that skylight up, that is if the others don't object, they mostly do – yes! – it is a bit stuffy – but you soon get used to it – what did you say? – there are no chairs – well, you can move some of your make-up over a bit and sit on the dressing bench. How many dress in this alley? Don't call it an alley – it's the gents dressing room – and all the principals use it – it generally holds about twenty – the star actors dress near the door and the rest move down one by one according to their position in the company – see! – those lines – painted on the wall – well, they represent a dressing space. What! Where are the mirrors? Oh, you find your own or borrow. Eh! What's that, how do the actors make-up who haven't got a gas-light on their section? They use candles stuck in beer bottles.

If you care to count you will find there are twenty-five dressing spaces, including the toilet arrangements at the end – follow me – and I will show you – this is it – I know there are no basins, but there's plenty of pails and a water tap, what more do you want – besides, isn't this portion of the pass – er – room, covered in zinc, and isn't there an overhead tap in case you would like a shower, isn't that enough? Good gracious, of course there is no hot water – what are you, a sybarite? Yes, I'll admit it is a bit trying in the

John Lupino as Pantaloon, 1822

Sara Lane as Jacqueline, 1840

Interior view of the Britannia Theatre, Hoxton

winter time – but you can, if you wish, heat a kettle on that gas ring. Now, what is it? What other toilet arrangements are there? – No – nothing except that pail painted red – that's – oh, come on! Do you see all those little grooves on the brick wall, where the red shows through the whitewash – well that's where the old actors used to scrape the brick to obtain red dust to use when they ran short of rouge – yes, it is rather smelly, but for goodness sake don't sniff in that fashion, you seem to forget that your grandfather and your great grandfather – and nearly all your relations spent the best part of twelve hours a day in this atmosphere; for years and years, dressing and undressing, eating, drinking and sleeping – yes, sleeping! Many's the time, when your grandfather and I have been too tired to go home to Tottenham, have we spent the night under the dressing bench on a bed of props, and slept soundly, too – so tired out with a ten hours pantomime – that even the rats didn't disturb us – turning your nose up, eh? Let me tell you my lad, that if you intend to ply the trade of a mummer, you won't always have the comfort of a Coliseum – don't forget, this was thirty years ago, and electric light, hot and cold running water and padded arm chairs, were not the usual fixtures of a dressing room – pros are pampered now and grumble if their dressing room is not carpeted and curtained, painted and decorated, with divans, cheval mirrors and wardrobes – they can even grumble if they are not on the stage level and have to share it with somebody else.

'What, one flight up – no carpet – no couch – no telephone – no toilet – what a hole!' Let me tell you, this old Brit dressing room was a palace to some places I've dressed in – I remember once that the whole troupe, including your grandmother and aunts, had to share a cellar beneath the stage with only a piece of old canvas dividing the men from the women – and we had to stand on a board placed upon bricks to prevent our feet from getting wet – even as near as a year or so ago, when I was the star of the show, owing to dressing room shortage – I had to dress in a converted Ladies – oh, come on!

Back again on the stage – look at those enormous wings, twenty-four feet wide and twenty-two feet high – they are the flats – how do the men handle them? Easily – do you see those great wooden shelves on the flys-level? Those with the deep wooden ruts on the underneath portion? Well, they are first lowered on a chain until they project out nearly to the centre of the stage, then the flat is placed in at one end and pushed along until it meets its fellow flat from the other side. They are called the grooves – no, you never see them now – they use back wings and cut cloths instead, personally, I think they could be re-introduced with advantage, for with this method you could get a firmly held scene, containing practical doors and windows – and it is much more effective to see a scene open from the centre – or close in slowly from the side, instead of dropping a cloth in a black out. That reminds me, I must tell you about 'Weaver' he was in charge of number one on the O.P. side. In his young days, when first placed in charge of this scenic effect, he was of slim and slender form, toward the latter end of his career – his latter end had become – to be polite – somewhat portly and prominent, the consequence was, that Weaver when moving his flat off, always managed to leave a portion of his posterior projecting beyond the edge of the wing – this exposure of his corduroy covered extremity was always the signal for a round of applause, which continued until it disappeared slowly from view. Weaver, or rather, what you could see of Weaver, was one of the 'outstanding' hits of the programme – of course he was quite unaware of his public appearance – and put the applause down to the artistic, even pace that he imparted to the change of scene – he used to tell the younger flat movers, 'Do it like me, boy! Then perhaps you'll get a hand.' 'Yus, that's all right, Weaver, but we can't.' Of course they couldn't, they were not built that way. Sometimes – but not when Burgess was about, the boys in the stalls would take pot shots with nuts at the slowly moving target, but without much success – for there is no record of anyone getting a bulls-eye – I may as well tell you, the audience who knew their Shakespeare, called him, 'Bottom The Weaver.'

George Lupino as a clown in Drury Lane, 1912

Now we will wander up to the back of the stage – a pretty good depth, eh? – over a hundred feet, – they don't build as deep now, usually the limit is about twenty-five – and the stages – they are only platforms, with no practicabilities at all – look at this stage – it is built with every conceivable trap you can imagine – stars, vamps, foot-first, bum first, head dives, cuts, floats, bridges and revolving sections – and just look up at the Grid! Over a hundred feet high and fitted with bridges, travelling sheaves, and all types of flying ballet effects – and did you ever see a fly floor like that – double decked, the lower fitted with over a dozen lime lights perches, either side – observe that enormous drum – that is built to carry any weight up to three tons – look at the space you have for stacking flats – the huge scene docks, at the back – there – there! Under that arch, why! That dock alone is bigger than the majority of the stages you play on nowadays – and just look at that mass of timber and iron in the corner, – that is machinery for effects off; – wind machines, thunder rolls, of all types, rain effects, glass crashes, earthquakes, sea effects, wind effects; artillery and gun fire of every description; – bird effects, from the domestic cock to the cuckoo; – animal effects, from the horse to the hyena; – and the property room – that one – is only a small temporary store place for hand props – the actual property room is an immense room or rather rooms, in those you can find anything from a bead to a battleship – can you find all this in your modern theatres? No! These days you are lucky if you can get a suite of second hand saddle bag furniture and a pop-gun; – and so you see that huge, iron bound wooden casing, stretching up into the flys? That is the great thunder roll. Up under the Grid are stacked dozens of cannon balls resting on an incline, when a lever is pulled, the balls, with a rumbling roar, roll down, with ever increasing speed, an iron covered rake, this encircles the entire auditorium and comes out on the opposite side of the stage – here the balls fall through a hole in the fly floor upon great iron plates in the cellar below. You can imagine the effect of the gradual rumble, rumble, getting louder and louder and the ear – splitting crash at

George Lupino as a clown in Drury Lane, 1912.
Father of G. B. Lupino Snr. and grandfather of G. B. Lupino Jnr.

the finish. It was impressive – well – picture in your mind a silent and attentive audience listening to little Elsie (perhaps you will recognise her under her better known name Lily Elsie – the Merry Widow). Well – picture her standing in the centre of the stage in a spotlight, singing a lullaby – ('Go to sleep my Baby' the song was) – the whole house was hushed – when Lily, who had reached the interesting climax per the medium of a high falsetto note, 'Baby has gone to sleep!' Then, rumble, rumbles, crash, bank, rumble, rumble, biff, bang, wallop – Crash!! – that is what happened, one night, many moons ago – Whew! – what an effect – what a row – who did it? – who did it? – who pulled the lever? Nobody seemed to know – but I remember Dad saying to Bigwood, 'All right Jimmy, I'll get to the bottom of this' – and he did -both of them.

And see – there's a cat, the image of the one your Uncle Mark trimmed with Harry Pleon's razor – what a howl that cat got, when I enticed him on the stage with a piece of cats meat, held in the jaws of my cats mask – What a howl that cat looked standing there in the full glare of the footlights, with its fur trimmed a la French poodle. What a howl! – but it was nothing to the howl that went up in the dressing room, when we both got belted on the buttock with the business end of a ballet shoe. – Whack! Whack! Whack! – that'll teach you to be kind to dumb animals – Whack! Whack! Whack! – but I'm ashamed to say it didn't – every animal in the theatre – and there were many – always gave us a wide berth – cats in particular.

There was one rat bitten old Tom – a tortoiseshell cat with filigree ears, who always kept his one eye open in case he was captured, placed in a hatbox and then sent up the star trap. Gee! How he would protest at this indignity to his cat-hood. But nevertheless, he performed this act time and time again – in fact so often was he captured and sent up, that eventually he discarded the stage and transferred his activities to the flys – where we could frequently see him looking down with a malevolent glare.

And look! There are two more – very similar to the pair that were placed tail to tail, – I am pleased to say in this instance we were not the culprits – poor cats! Some of the boys placed the cats back to back, wrapped their tails around with some of the electricians insulating tape, then threw them on the stage to decide between themselves who was to be the leader – poor cats – after this affray they were itemized among the cat stocks, as Manx.

Ah! There's the old wine vat that formed the kennel of the night watchman's dog: a bull terrier known as Romeo, whose ears, and tail, and other portions of the anatomy, we so often decorated with tin foil, and gold leaf – poor, ill-used old dog – who could never understand, after we had placed a pin on the nose end of his muzzle, why all his affinities refused to flirt.

That recess in the wall, next to Romeo's residence, is 'Niffy's Nook' – but first I had better tell you who Niffy was; officially, he was the night watchman, and deputy stage door keeper – and what is known in this locality as a 'cough drop' in other words, 'a bit of a lad' – a 'character'.

As he remains clearer in my memory than any other members of the staff, and he was connected with an outstanding episode in the theatre, Niffy shall have the stage alone.

– Presenting –
'Niffy the Night Owl'

In figure, Niffy was decidedly of the dachshund breed – long bodies and short, decidedly bandy legged – in face – what you could see of it for whiskers, florid; – the whiskers were of an undecided Airedale red, and his head, was a bare as a billiard ball.

Protruding from the forest of whiskers, was a Roman nose, very rugged and ruddy – and mostly in an incipient state of hay fever. This organ had a peculiar habit of palpitating at the base line – somewhat in the manner of a rabbit, probably this nasal peculiarity was the reason for his nickname, 'Niffy.'

What his actual name was I never knew, and I think there is

a strong possibility that through answering to Niffy for so many years, he had forgotten it himself. In addition to the external peculiarities already recorded, Niffy possessed a voice, that was, if not sweet, decidedly low, in fact he had no voice to speak of, and to be perfectly honest, very little to speak with, a cold contracted when a youth, had left him with a chronic laryngitis – so he was really, a 'whispering watchman.'

When he wished to communicate with anyone he would seize them by the lapel of the coat, and bark hoarse, staccato noises into their ear, exuding at the same time that much used East End scent 'Parfum de Watney's Entire.' This will give you some slight impression of our principal character.

Niffy in his official capacity, seemed to spend the greater part of his career, sitting on a stool in a cubby hut in a state of semi-somnolence, and it was only by a close inspection of his nasal action, that one could tell that he was alive.

Occasionally he would come out of his comatose condition and roam round the building accompanied by Romeo, the bull terrier. After his 'round' he would return to the aforementioned cubby hut for his nightly nap.

The hut must now occupy our attention, for it forms a prominent prop in the production. It was of the sentry box type, huge, cumbersome, and extremely heavy, padded both inside and out with leather. Originally it had been a janitors hall box seat, of the early Georgian period, and had been used in its early days in the theatre, as stage decoration in many of the period plays that were produced there; but, becoming too old and dilapidated to use as a prop, besides being too heavy and cumbersome, it had been discarded and relegated to the scrap heap.

Niffy, scenting a comfortable and snug retreat, had reclaimed this ancient relic and had it transplanted to the cellar below the stage.

The part of the cellar he had chosen was extremely quiet, used mostly by the supers, who were in the main, relics of the palmy

Four-year-old G. B. Lupino with his father and company c. 1920. *From the back, left to right*: Uncle Wally, Uncle Stanley, Uncle Harry, Barry Lupino Jnr., George Lupino (Barry's grandad), Lupino Lane, Barry Lupino Snr., Uncle Mark.

days of the drama, their youthful hose, well saved, a world too wide for their shrunk shank, who objected strenuously in their childish treble, and with many pipe and whistling sound, to Niffy's presence in their sacred domain; but Niffy won the day and became a temporary tenant, planting his sentry box in a small archway that led into a larger cellar below the paint room floor.

Here, by the spluttering light of a solitary gas jet, protected by a bent and blackened wire guard, he made his headquarters, snug and secure from interruption or interference.

Niffy's pet aversion was 'boys!' – especially the boys attached to the theatre, of which there were many. This species of humanity usually appeared in the pantomimes as elves, gnomes, goblins and devils, – Niffy's publicly expressed opinion was that they played their parts naturally.

'Ruddy little pests, ought not to be allowed in the theatre, h'upsetting everybody and everything – Wot do you think the ruddy little rats did yesterday? – Why – they filled the mouthpiece of me clay pipe up with bitter Haloes! – Ruddy, rotten little rates.'

If there existed an armed neutrality between the lean and slippered supers and himself, open warfare was rife between the boys and Niffy – and both parties had to be wary of an ambush or a sudden raid.

Sometimes Niffy would pretend to be asleep, then suddenly pounce out from his hut, seize a stray member of the boys brigade and – Swish! Swish! would go his cane, right across the boy's beam, until the howls of the injured one would bring reinforcements, then, back he would go and barricade himself in behind Romeo's snarling teeth.

At times he would wait until the troupe were lined up in their dresses and masks waiting to go on, then, as they dared not retaliate, because the Super Master was present – Niffy would slyly sneak behind them and get in a stealthy pin prick or a pinch on a boy's posterior. – It was no use protesting, as the Super Master privately endorsed Niffy's opinion that they were 'Ruddy little pests.' Needless to say, Mark and I, were numbered among these 'pests' – in fact, Niffy said, the two Lupino kids were the ringleaders and by far the worst.

Didn't they shove the 'addock into the bass fiddle – and cause half the band to complain that the drains wanted seeing to – didn't they fill the stage manager's speaking tube full of soot, so as when 'e blew down it, 'e 'arf smothered the conductor. – Well, if it wasn't them two, who was it? – tell me that – blasted little brats! – Who was it that soaped the fiddle strings? – them two! – who broke the stink bomb in the 'orses dress? and made the two h'actors fight like fury inside ' – them two! Them two! Who put the cow itch in me 'elmet – them two!

Yes! No matter what went wrong or what happened, it was always – them two!

Even when the fowls in the farmyard scene were found one day apparently dead, and were promptly plucked by a parsimonious property man, and then some hours afterwards were discovered very much alive, running round the room crowing like fury without a feather to fly with – them two got the blame, until it was found out that the heap of grain from which they were fed, had been stored in the wine cellar for months, soaking up the seepage from the rum casks – and the poor chickens were only blind paralytic drunk, instead of dead, when just discovered. Poor fowls, how self-conscious and they naked looked running round in the nude.

However – to continue with Niffy – at odd times he would relieve the day stage door keeper at the back door – and then it was, the boys had to be particularly alert, for in a hundred different ways he would try to make their life a misery – his great opportunity being when they signed the register, then he would rap them over the knuckles with a ruler, or kick them down the stairs as they passed. At times he would change his tactics and pretend to be friendly, but this was only when he required a message running, such as popping over to the Lion for a pint of 'the usual', but he gave this up when he discovered that the boys had played a practical joke on him – 'Wot do yer think them pests did? – put some jalap in me beer'. After this experience he usually came on duty plentifully supplied and this he placed on a shelf in the door keepers office – but the boys – 'them two' as usual, found out that they could get at it through a hole in the roof, and with the assistance of a thin tube of gas piping, they managed to doctor the beverage frequently.

Niffy couldn't understand it at all, 'the blinking beer's got a 'orrid taste lately, can't make it out – me stomic 'as gone back on me'. Eventually he gave the beer up and went on a diet of rum – this being kept in a bottle with a corked top – he recovered.

Another trick of his, was to hide behind the little windows of the stage door office, wait until the boys were all gathered in a group waiting to go in at the 'half hour', then he would suddenly open the window and throw the dregs from his tea can all over them, and pretend it was an accident.

Talking about throwing things out, reminds me of throwing things in – this episode is connected with your Uncle Mark – as you know, Uncle Mark has a peculiar humorous and nonchalant way of being personal in his remarks and also in his actions – when in this mood nothing seems to disturb his cherub like calm, and this yarn, will show that the child was father to the man.

One day – as Uncle Mark was waiting to go in with the rest of the boys – (he would be about twelve years old at the time) – a tall dignified stranger came to him and said, – (the stranger by the way, was Roy Redgrave, reporting for the first time) – 'Tell me, my boy, which is the Britannia Theatre, Hoxton? – and where can I find a person known as Niffy?'

Mark, after eyeing the stranger up and down, while the rest of the boys stood round, slowly pointed to the building and said, very slowly and distinctly, 'That's the Brit.' Next without hurrying the action, he indicated the stage door, 'That's the stage door.' Swinging his finger slowly around he pointed to the window, 'That's the window of Niffy's office.' Then stooping down he picked up a stone and with slow and deliberate aim, threw it through the window, the

Barry Lupino, Snr. in the 1920s

Barry Lupino, Jnr. c. 1934

George Lupino, 1926, just before his last appearance. From a painting by Philip Ledoux

Mrs Barry Lupino in the 1920s

glass broke with a startling crash, instantly, the old man, his face purple with rage, appeared at the ruined window – 'and that,' Mark concluded, imperturbably, 'is Niffy.'

We will now introduce you to another member of the cast, namely, the stage door keeper, one, Mike, better known as 'Skin the Goat' – subsequently shortened to 'Skinny.' He was an Irish cockney and suspected of Fenian sympathies – hence, 'Skin the Goat.' For your edification – 'Skin the Goat' was a notorious Fenian of the mid-Victorian age.

Now for 'Skinny'. He was a tall, cadaverous, lantern jawed individual, who always wore, tightly wrapped around his throat, a highly coloured choker with the ends securely fastened to his braces, these were of leather, (which he frequently used, as a razor strop) and helped to support a pair of pants of a shade known in art circles as 'Beige', the buttons or fastenings of the said pants had mostly burst from their anchorage, and the canvas that had originally added to their security, usually protruded from there with a forlorn aspect of neglect; in case of emergency, a highly polished black belt, with a shiny brass S hook, decorated his waist line – his shirt was for ever of that 'tint' known as 'Army Grey' – his coat and vest, – whenever he wore them – were of a pepper and salt colour; in foot covering he favoured the type known as 'sneakers' and for head covering 'a sporting check', – this I think completes his sartorial effects, with the exception of a pair of highly polished brown puttees, which he was said to have worn at the Battle of Cressy![9]

Oh! I forgot to mention he wore a brightly sueted quiff and a Kitchener moustache which, Harry Pleon said, 'sapped his strength.'

'Skinny' was extremely excitable and argumentative, and possessed a flow of language that would place an Australian sheep shearer in the 'also ran' class; he could say more cuss words in a given time that anyone I have ever heard, including Phil Ray, and

9 Also known as the Battle of Crecy, this was the first of three English victories during the Edwardian phase of the Hundred Years' War.

The final rehearsal of the show in the Tiny Theatre c. 1929.
From left to right: June Lupino, Tonie Lupino, Ida Lupino, James Longstaff, Billie Stone, Barry Lupino Jnr., Marcie Stone, Laurie Lane, Doris Rudd, Rita Lupino.
Kneeling: Stanley Lupino.

it was suspected that he could curse in three languages at one time.

Unlike Niffy, he was extremely fond of the boys, and nearly always carried in his trousers pockets, a bag of Rowlands Cough Cures, which he would distribute – if he were able to prize them apart – to the boys as they entered. He and Niffy were deadly enemies and whenever they met – which only occurred when Niffy was relieving him at the stage door – there was always a row.

Skinny with lurid language accusing Niffy of upsetting his office. 'The blankety blank' place wants fumigating after you've used it you bewhiskered old skunk, why don't you cut that stinking, blinking goat hair off yer dirty dial? Yer blinkety – old blinker – you've had that 'air so long the blankety blank stuff is decayin' yer,' etc, etc.

Listening to this exchange of cross talk was one of our favourite amusements. Skinny in his high pitched falsetto voice, rattling off a ceaseless flow of personal comments; and Niffy, barking back like a boarhound with the croup, trying to get a word in edgeways; it invariably ended in Niffy making a heated exit into the office and slamming the door, where, from behind the glass window his bearded chin could be seen working at top speed.

Skinny, 'mid the cheers of the spectators, walking away with his jaw jerking nineteen to the dozen, stopping every few feet to hurl back an invective or so, he had overlooked in the recent debate. When Niffy thought Skinny was safely round the corner, he would run out and bark all kinds of threats; once he came running out, and tripped over a boy's foot and scooted about ten feet on his stomach finished up in the gutter, where he lay face downwards spitting out expletives and bits of mud. On this occasion, Skinny returned and promptly planted his plimsole right on Niffy's pants. This led to a fight. The whole staff downed tools and came running out, and after a lot of argument it was decided the lads were to fight it out Queenberry style, – a ring was formed – and the men toed the scratch – Niffy favoured the Jeffery crouch – Skinny's style was a cross between an electric fan and Pavlova.

Round One

The men rushed to a clinch, wherein fighting of the Cumberland and Westmorland style took place.[10] Skinny, with a left hook and the flying mare, had his man on the canvas. Niffy took a count of nine on his hip, on rising he tried the La Blanche pirouette blow, but was cautioned by the referee. End of round one. Skinny's round on account of foot work.

Round Two

Both men rushed for a clinch – but missed, both took a short count. Niffy, with a rabbit killer, got home on Skinny's clay pipe, which he had forgotten to remove – Skinny took a count and half an ounce of shag out of his mouth – with a right hook he got a hammer lock on Niffy's whiskers, the excitement was intense. Niffy broke away

10 Referring to the Cumberland and Westmorland Yeomanry – a Yeomanry Calvary Regiment formed in 1819.

Our Home painted by George Lupino, 1915

Some of the Lupino clan c. 1927.
Seated: Lupino Lane, Harry Lupino, George Lupino, Barry Lupino
Standing: Wallace Lupino, Mark Lupino, Stanley Lupino.

and started to spar at arm's length – the men were now exchanging word for word. Niffy was evidently looking for an opening – at last he saw it – the stage door; so with a yell he made for it, went in and slammed it behind him. 'The Battle of the Brit' was over – Skinny was left in possession of the field and a handful of whiskers.

Yes! Skinny was a fighter, right from the day the doctor said, 'It's a boy!'

* * *

One morning, the stage staff, coming to work, found a fuming and furious Skinny kicking his heels and chunks off the stage door, outside the building – 'what s'matter, Skinny?' 'Matter?' yelled Skinny, frantic and half frozen; that bald-headed, bandy-legged, son of Simian Niffy, 'as gone 'ome and taken the blankly ruddy key with him, 'ere 'av I been standing outside colling my gory carcass the best part of a hour, blast the be-whiskered old basket – bumper.'

After knocking for some time, but getting no answer, they finally forced their way in and upon going into the paint room they discovered that a big wooden wheel, used for winding up the huge paint frames, had broken from its moorings and had fallen right through the paint room into the cellar below.

Repairing the damage occupied their attention the best part of the day. So Niffy's home going was not thought of. That night the show went on as usual, as shows have a habit of doing, no matter what accidentally may occur, and the hour arrived for Niffy to take over from Skinny – but ten o'clock came and went and no Niffy! This only served to feed the wrath of Skinny, who was still smarting over being locked out in the morning – eleven o'clock – twelve – twelve-thirty – but still no sign of Niffy. Everybody went home, leaving Skinny almost semi-speechless with rage, to put in some overtime, minding the theatre.

As they say in the movies:

The staff arrived as usual, but this time, instead of a cursing, fuming fanatic, they found a very subdued and scared Skinny, pale as a parsnip and practically petrified with fright. 'Boys,' he gasped out, 'thank 'eavens you've come. I've never 'ad sich a night in me life – the blinking Brit's 'aunted – Ghosts! – I tell yer – 'orrible, 'owling ghosts! – I wouldn't spend a night 'ere again for a 'undred Niffy's. No, not for all the beer in Burton – it's 'aunted, that's wot it is.'

At five o'clock that same afternoon, a tall, funereal female came to the stage door and said to Skinny; 'Is Niffy in?' 'No, the old rat ain't in,' replied Skinny. 'Why?'

'Well, I'm 'is widow,' answered the woman. 'Wot? 'is widow?' shrieked the startled Skinny. 'His widow!! No – I ain't 'is wife, thank 'eavens,' said the woman with the sniff – 'I'm the widow wot he boards with – but 'e ain't been 'ome, so I got a bit anxious about me bill – and called round to see if 'e'd 'opped it.'

'Wot! Niffy ain't been 'ome neither? I wonder where the be-whiskered old brute got to? Blimey! – I wonder if he's under that stuff that fell down in the paint room. Blimey!! 'Aary! 'Aary!!' With that, Skinny rushed in, followed by the widow; and in a few moments the whole staff, assisted by various Hoxtonites, who had been hanging around the stage door, began to search for Niffy. Someone broke the glass to the fire alarm – and soon two engines and a ladder brigade turned up to help in the search. A curious crowd gathered, as crowds will if something strange is happening – coster mongers left their stalls to hang around the stage door – the police arrived to keep the crowd back, rumours flew from mouth to mouth – Skinny had murdered Niffy, and they were bringing the body out, an ambulance turned up and was retained for future use; the crowed increased, more police were sent for, another brigade arrived, by this time it was 'Niffy who had murdered Skinny and had run away with his widow.' Hoxton was in uproar. Inside the theatre, the firemen, and the other helpers were working frantically to move the smashed and broken scenery in the paint room cellar, eventually the debris was removed, but no sign of 'Niffy' echoed through the building. It was taken up by the crowd outside, all that could be heard was, 'Niffy!' Niffy!! Niffy!!! People attracted by the noise began to run from Shoreditch, Kingsland, Haggerston, Highgate, Halifax, the Hebrides, the Far East, here, there, and everywhere.

The crowd became so dense that somebody suggested sending for the Tower Hamlets, the rumour now was the widow had now committed suicide, murdered Skinny, and they were bringing the body out. The theatre was a seething mass of firemen on the roof, in the cellar, in the bar, everywhere, – but still no trace of Niffy – not even of Niffy's chair – not even a hair of Niffy's dog – not even a Niff!!

The crowd were becoming restless – calling for action – and Niffy! – Ladders were run up inside the building, ladders were run up inside the building – ladders were running up everywhere – even in the firemens hose; – the rumour had now changed to 'Niffy had married the widow, committed harri-karri and they were bringing the building out. 'Eventually some of the searchers went down a sharp incline that led from the stage cellar under the orchestra, into a huge vault beneath the pit floor, where the whiskey and beer casks were stored, and there by the dim light of the firemens' lantern they found – laying face downward on the floor – no – not Niffy – Niffy's chair.

There it lay – the huge cumbersome sentry box hut – there it lay in a pool of – surely not – a closer scrutiny proved it to be nothing but seepage from the numerous vats and casks. A sigh of relief – coupled with a certain amount of regret went up among the crowd. But where is Niffy! Someone suggested leaving the beer cellar. But Skinny, for some reason refused. The vault was searched, the walls were tapped, so were the barrels, but no signs of Niffy! The doors were tried – the taps also – but still no sign – just as somebody suggested going for a corkscrew a strange wailing sound sighed

G. B.Lupino Snr. in character c. 1935

through the cellar – with a gulp, Skinny almost swallowed the bottle, and with a piercing shriek, the widow fainted – they all rushed to bring her too – no, they didn't bring her another – that's too old – Again that strange sound, it seemed to have come from the very bowels of the earth – someone gasped, 'It's under the chair,' with uncertain steps they tiptoed toward the sinister-looking thing and listened with tongues hanging out. Again! That peculiar saxophone sob – the widow began to weep – she was well away; with the trembling hands they slowly lifted the heavy cumbersome chair – and there – with his whiskers soaking up the seepage, and his head reclining on Romeo the rat hound soused to the nostrils, lay Niffy – Picture!

– Slow Curtain –

Epilogue on Niffy's Narrative

When Niffy had recovered sufficiently to articulate without hiccoughing – which did not happen for nearly a week – he told the following, thrilling story. In his own words, it ran something like this:

> H'it was like this 'ere – about h'eight in the morning, I done me usual round with Romeo, and 'ad just settled down in the 'ut to 'ave a quiet read of the 'H'eaven-ing Noose' when h'all of a sudden I 'eard an 'orrible crash, an' then the blinkin' 'ut shot through the h'air as h'if a h'earthquake 'ad 'it h'it – an next thing I knowed was, I knowed nothin'. When I came to, there I was layin' on me stumick with me 'ed on top of Romeo, and the blinkin' 'ut on top of me. As soon as I got on to the 'amg of things I naturally tried to lift the 'ut h'up, but the blinking thing was too 'eavy, so I starts 'ollering – Well, yer knows wot me 'obsons[11] is like, don't yer – so I soon threw that h'up and 'ad another go at lifting – first I 'ad a go at layin' on me back

[11] 'Hobson's choice' is Cockney rhyming slang for 'voice'.

Barry Lupino Jnr. producing *Judge for Yourself* at the BBC

and tryin' to h'elervate 'er with me feet – but me stomock was in the way, so I turns h'over an' tried kneelin' an' liftin' 'er with me back – but the blinking thing was so 'eavy I could h'only h'elervate 'er about a couple of h'inches, so I 'ad to drop h'it – then Romeo turned nasty 'cos I dropped h'it h'on 'is foot. So I 'ad another go at hollering.

Well, I 'ollered and 'owled and 'owled and 'ollered, until I realised that the place was h'empty, – so I decided to make the best of bad job till the boys turned h'up in the morning, so I pushed Romeo h'up to the h'end made meself as comfortable as possible and 'ad a nap.

Next thing I 'eard was Skinny, 'ammering at the stage door – and 'ollering for me ter let 'im in, so I 'ollered back, but wot with me being 'id in the cellar and h'under the 'ut an' all, and me 'obsons being 'oarse through 'owling for h'over a hour – 'e couldn't 'ear me.

Next thing I 'eard was the boys moving about h'in the paint room, so started 'ollering again, but they made sich a 'orrid row moving the scenery, they couldn't 'ear me either.

Then I started to 'ammer on the h'inside of the 'ut with me 'and, but it 'urt, so I threw that h'up – then I 'ad a go at kicking with me feet, but I 'urt me 'eels and besides there wasn't much room to swing me feet h'in, so I turned that h'in, and 'ad a go at pinching Romeo, to try an' make 'im bark, but the unthankful 'ound bit me on the h'ankle. H'all this time I could 'ear the boys working away quite close to me, so h'every now and again I would h'eleverate the'ut an h'inch or so, and give another 'oller but I got 'oarser and 'oarser until I couldn't 'oller no longer. Then I 'ad another go at lifting the 'ut and by a h'effort I got it h'up about six h'inches but the bally thing slid forward.

This gives me an h'idea! So I thought, that if I could move the 'ut forward a bit at a time – I might get nearer to where the boys were working; and them seeing a moving 'ut – they would lift h'it h'up and rescue me.

So orft I starts on me trip – at first Romeo give me a bit of trouble 'cos he would keep getting 'is tail trapped, but after a bit 'e cottons on to the h'idea and keeps out of the way.

Of co'rs, all this was 'ard work, the blinking 'ut was 'eavy – and me being h'inside I couldn't see where I was going – h'all I 'ad to work on was me sense of 'earing.

Well, I must 'ave been at this for hours, walking h'on me knees, h'elervating the 'ut with me back – and then letting 'er slide forward h'inches at a time – I felt like a blinking Trocadero walking along in 'is shell.

H'after a bit, things became quiet – so I come to the conclusion the boys 'ad gone to dinner – then I got 'ungry but of c'orse I 'ad nothing to eat in the 'ut so I 'ad a chew terbacco and a good long rest. When the boys come back, h'off I starts again, but it was 'ard work and the 'eat h'inside the 'ut was 'orrible and soon I was h'expiring from every core. I'm not kidding you when I tells yer, I was covered in beads of consternation from 'ed to 'eels.

Suddenly I 'its something and the 'ole 'ut swings round and gets wedged, and 'ow long it took me to get a move on again I don't know – I know Romeo starts to get restless so I judged it was about time for 'is usual run, so I get a bit anxious.

Then I 'eard the band a'tuning in, so I gets desperate and starts 'ollering again – but the blinking drums drowned me voice, so I 'as another go at lifting the 'ut and then, suddenly the old lot slides forward down a 'ill or something with a bump and stops.

Then something starts to h'ooze h'under the h'edge and I 'ad a vision of being drowned like a rat in a trap – but it stops suddenly – so I gives Romeo a clip over the lug to ease me feelings. After a bit it starts to soak into me pants and I began to wonder wot it could be, so I puts the tip of me finger in it and 'eld it to me nose – it smelled like beer – it was beer! Of co'rse I took advantage of the opportunity and quenches me thirst and then, – wot with the 'eat and the h'efforts – I swooned. Anyways when I recovers a bit I tried to think out wot was the best thing to do, I tried to think wot the miners did when they were h'embalmed – but it h'upset me – then I got 'ungry – so I 'ad a go at Romeo's bone – 'e 'ad brought with 'im, but 'e got the needle – so I threw that h'up and Romeo eats it 'imself, but it was soaked h'in beer – so 'e threw h'it up – then I 'ad a brain wave an' thought of the

> little side windows in the 'ut. So I broke one of them with me boot – puts me arm out of the 'ole,and I found a can 'anging on a nail – I brought it in the 'ut and found it was full of something that smelled like rum – and then I knowed no more.

What had actually happened was this; the big wooden wheel that had broken from the paint roof in falling had rolled against the hut and knocked it over – but though this was thoroughly explained to him, Niffy for ever afterwards had a deep-rooted suspicion that it was the work of 'them two.'

Writing all this is pretty tiresome. Having to read it must be something simply terrible. So this is where it ends.

All my love, Dad,

Barry Lupino.

G. B. Lupino Snr. in his later years in the 1950s

AFTERWORD

My relationship with the Lupino family commenced at eleven years old when I appeared with them in a pantomime in Brighton in 1945–46 in which several members of the family were involved. On one occasion, I was permitted to stand quietly in the wings to watch the Dame Barry Lupino Snr., performing 'butterfly turns and leaps' all around the stage. This was amazing, especially as he was in his sixties. I did not meet Barry Lupino Jnr. until seven years later when he worked for the BBC as an executive producer. I worked for both the BBC and ITV as a dancer and choreographer and our paths crossed frequently. We married in 1960, and having nine children insures the Lupino legacy will continue well into the future.

With regard to the contents of the chest, it is held safely at the Victoria and Albert museum in London. However, the letter remains the property of and in the possession of the Lupino family.

In the production of this book, special thanks must be given to the Victoria and Albert museum for their kind support, family and friends and in particular, my youngest daughter, Anna, and her husband, Richard Wishart, for their persistence and dogged determination in getting this book published.

Janet Lupino

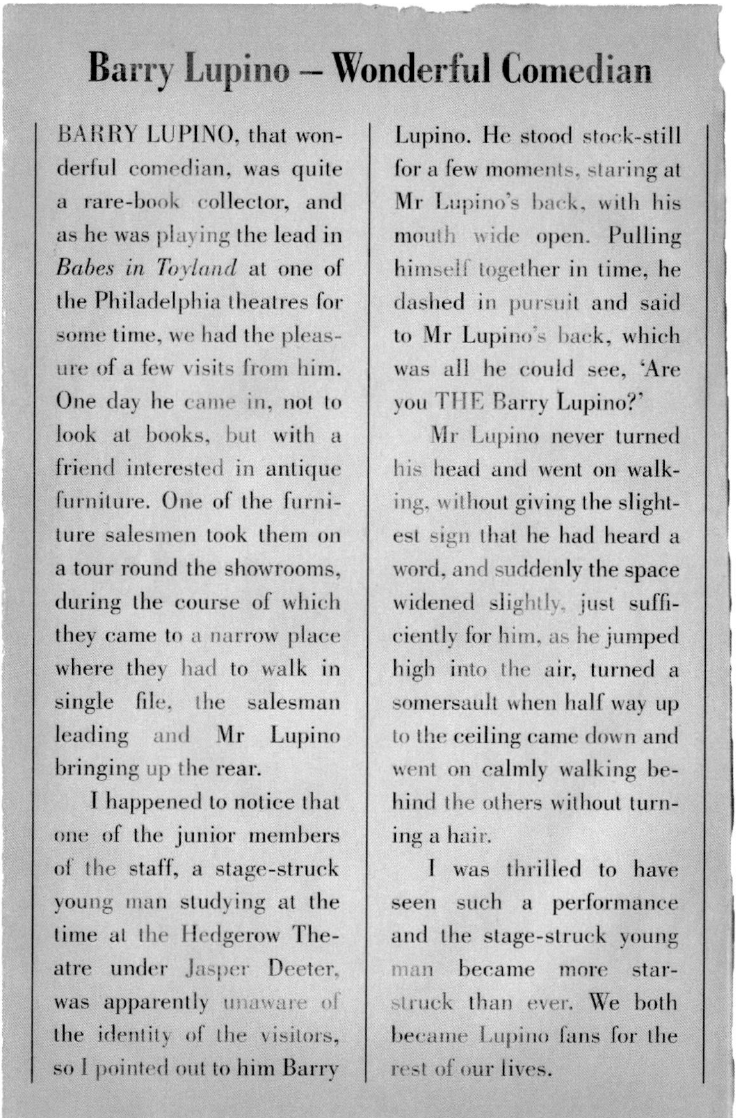
Barry Lupino – Wonderful Comedian

BARRY LUPINO, that wonderful comedian, was quite a rare-book collector, and as he was playing the lead in *Babes in Toyland* at one of the Philadelphia theatres for some time, we had the pleasure of a few visits from him. One day he came in, not to look at books, but with a friend interested in antique furniture. One of the furniture salesmen took them on a tour round the showrooms, during the course of which they came to a narrow place where they had to walk in single file, the salesman leading and Mr Lupino bringing up the rear.

I happened to notice that one of the junior members of the staff, a stage-struck young man studying at the time at the Hedgerow Theatre under Jasper Deeter, was apparently unaware of the identity of the visitors, so I pointed out to him Barry Lupino. He stood stock-still for a few moments, staring at Mr Lupino's back, with his mouth wide open. Pulling himself together in time, he dashed in pursuit and said to Mr Lupino's back, which was all he could see, 'Are you THE Barry Lupino?'

Mr Lupino never turned his head and went on walking, without giving the slightest sign that he had heard a word, and suddenly the space widened slightly, just sufficiently for him, as he jumped high into the air, turned a somersault when half way up to the ceiling came down and went on calmly walking behind the others without turning a hair.

I was thrilled to have seen such a performance and the stage-struck young man became more star-struck than ever. We both became Lupino fans for the rest of our lives.

An article written in appreciation of Barry Lupino Snr. which it is understood to have been published at the approximate time that the letter was written to his son.

ROYAL FAMILY OF GREASE PAINT

EST. 1600

INDEX

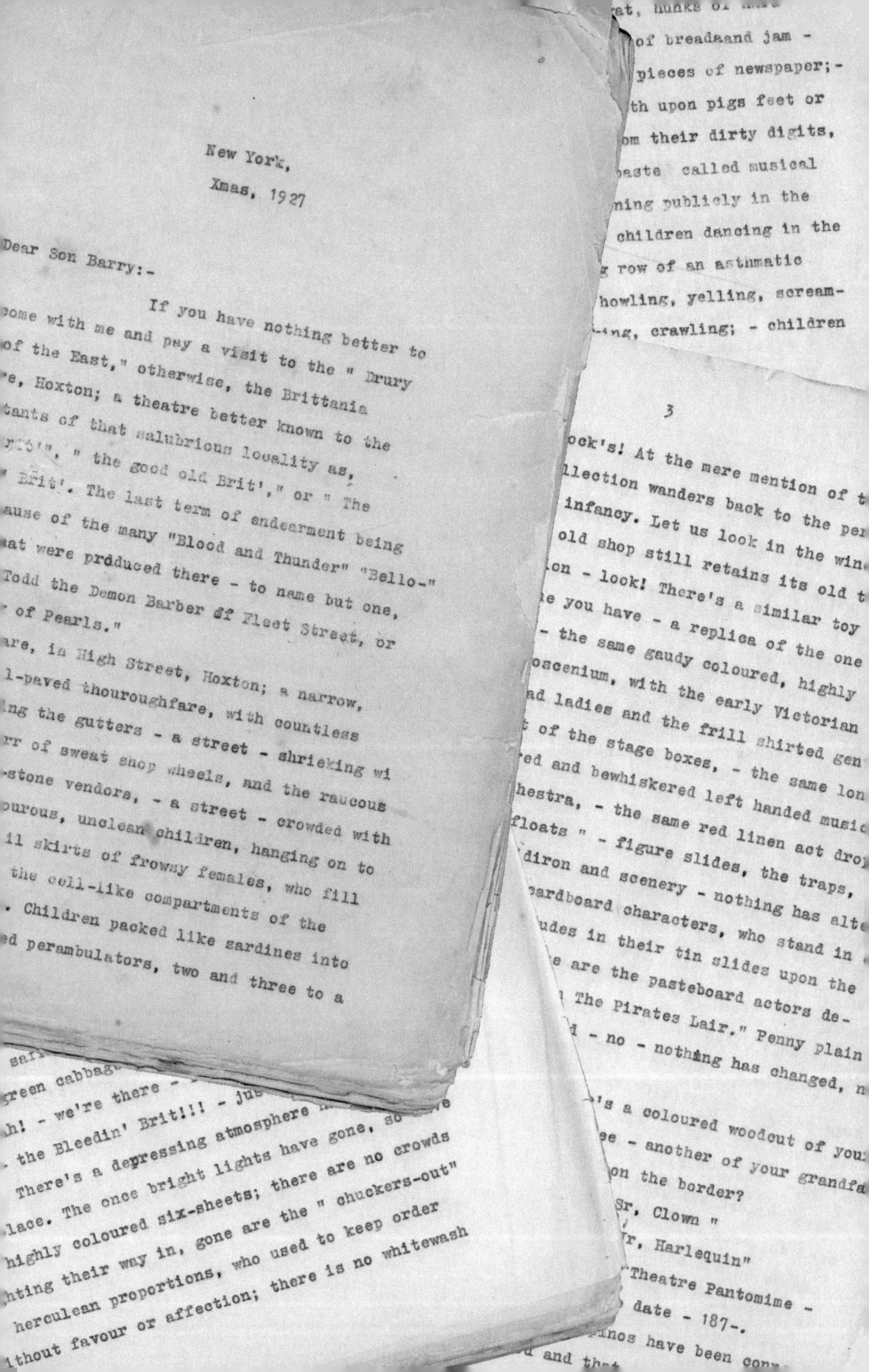

New York,

Xmas, 1927

Dear Son Barry:-

If you have nothing better to
come with me and pay a visit to the " Drury
of the East," otherwise, the Brittania
e, Hoxton; a theatre better known to the
tants of that salubrious locality as,
rit'", " the good old Brit'," or " The
Brit'. The last term of endearment being
ause of the many "Blood and Thunder" "Bello-"
at were produced there - to name but one,
Todd the Demon Barber of Fleet Street, or
of Pearls."
are, in High Street, Hoxton; a narrow,
l-paved thouroughfare, with countless
ng the gutters - a street - shrieking wi
rr of sweat shop wheels, and the raucous
-stone vendors, - a street - crowded with
purous, unclean children, hanging on to
il skirts of frowsy females, who fill
the cell-like compartments of the
. Children packed like sardines into
ed perambulators, two and three to a

at, hunks of
of breadaand jam -
pieces of newspaper;-
th upon pigs feet or
om their dirty digits,
paste called musical
ning publicly in the
children dancing in the
g row of an asthmatic
howling, yelling, scream-
ing, crawling; - children

3

ock's! At the mere mention of t
llection wanders back to the per
infancy. Let us look in the win
old shop still retains its old t
on - look! There's a similar toy
e you have - a replica of the one
- the same gaudy coloured, highly
oscenium, with the early Victorian
ad ladies and the frill shirted gen
t of the stage boxes, - the same lon
red and bewhiskered left handed music
hestra, - the same red linen act dro
floats " - figure slides, the traps,
diron and scenery - nothing has alte
ardboard characters, who stand in
udes in their tin slides upon the
e are the pasteboard actors de-
The Pirates Lair." Penny plain
d - no - nothing has changed, n
's a coloured woodcut of you
ee - another of your grandfa
on the border?
Sr, Clown "
Mr, Harlequin"
"Theatre Pantomime -
date - 187-.
inos have been con
d and that

sar
green cabbage
h! - we're there -
the Bleedin' Brit!!! - jus
There's a depressing atmosphere
lace. The once bright lights have gone, so
highly coloured six-sheets; there are no crowds
hting their way in, gone are the " chuckers-out"
herculean proportions, who used to keep order
ithout favour or affection; there is no whitewash